For Jared, who shared his universe with me
—KAF

For Mom, who taught me how to view my first
eclipse from our small drafty attic
—KL

ABOUT THIS BOOK

The illustrations for this book were created digitally. This book was edited by Deirdre Jones, art directed by David Caplan, and designed by Prashansa Thapa. The production was supervised by Kimberly Stella, and the production editor was Marisa Finkelstein. The text was set in Perpetua, and the display type is Linotype Centennial and Futura.

Text copyright © 2023 by Kathleen Fox • Illustrations copyright © 2023 by Khoa Le • Cover illustration 2023 by Khoa Le • Cover design by Prashansa Thapa • Cover copyright © 2023 by Hachette Book Group, Inc. • Hachette Book Group supports the right to free expression and the value of copyright. The purpose of copyright is to encourage writers and artists to produce the creative works that enrich our culture. • The scanning, uploading, and distribution of this book without permission is a theft of the author's intellectual property. If you would like permission to use material from the book (other than for review purposes), please contact permissions@hbgusa.com. Thank you for your support of the author's rights. • Little, Brown and Company • Hachette Book Group • 1290 Avenue of the Americas, New York, NY 10104 • Visit us at LBYR.com • First Edition: September 2023 • Little, Brown and Company is a division of Hachette Book Group, Inc. • The Little, Brown name and logo are trademarks of Hachette Book Group, Inc. • The publisher is not responsible for websites (or their content) that are not owned by the publisher. • Little, Brown and Company books may be purchased in bulk for business, educational, or promotional use. For information, please contact your local bookseller or the Hachette Book Group Special Markets Department at special.markets@hbgusa.com. • Library of Congress Cataloging-in-Publication Data • Names: Fox, Kate Allen, author. | Le, Khoa, 1982– illustrator. • Title: A few beautiful minutes : experiencing a solar eclipse / by Kate Allen Fox ; illustrated by Khoa Le. • Description: First edition. | New York, NY : Little, Brown and Company, 2023. | Includes bibliographical references. | Audience: Ages 4–8 | Summary: "Sky gazers experience a total solar eclipse in this descriptive picture book about the wonders of this phenomenon"— Provided by publisher. • Identifiers: LCCN 2022019891 | ISBN 9780316416924 (hardcover) • Subjects: LCSH: Solar eclipses—Juvenile literature. • Classification: LCC QB541.5 .F68 2023 | DDC 523.7/8—dc23/eng20221025 • LC record available at https://lccn.loc.gov/2022019891 • ISBN 978-0-316-41692-4 • PRINTED IN CHINA • APS • 10 9 8 7 6 5 4 3 2

A Few Beautiful Minutes

Experiencing a Solar Eclipse

Written by **Kate Allen Fox**

Illustrated by **Khoa Le**

Little, Brown and Company

New York   Boston

Under a broad, blue sky
from coast to coast,
we gather for a rare illusion . . .

a *total solar eclipse*—
when the sun vanishes into thin air

. . . for a few beautiful minutes.

In the endless expanse of space,
the universe prepares for a show,
one the sun and moon have given us
since the dawn of time.

They find their places
as the performance begins.

The sun, forever the star,
beams vast and vibrant,
her stage unchanged.

But the moon has already begun
gliding,
    sliding,
        slipping
        into the spotlight
        to steal the sun's glory

        . . . for a few beautiful minutes.

Little by little,
she hides the sun.

Our eyes alone can't see the change.
The sun, still too bright,
can burn them for life.

So we look through our sun viewers
and see that the glowing giant seems shrunken,
her circle chipped into a crescent.

In the shadows of trees,
slivers of light mirror
the sun's shifting silhouette.

The moon moves
farther and farther
in front of the sun.

A small sphere striving
to overshadow a giant
. . . for a few beautiful minutes.

Moment by moment,
for an hour or more,
the stage transforms.

The sun grows slimmer,
the sky dimmer,
as a midday twilight takes shape.

The world grows more dark than light
as eerie orange hues hug the horizon.

Above us, the sky becomes
as dark as the deep sea.
Stars, shining brighter than ever,
twinkle in that darkness.

Birds roost for the night
as crickets and bats wake.
Temperatures plummet
as the chill of night nips at our ears.

In the cold,
in the dark,
in anticipation,
we wait

     . . . for those few beautiful minutes.

The last rays of light fade away,
and the moment arrives.

The *corona*—
the sun's atmosphere or *crown*—
now shimmers round the moon,
the unlikely queen of the solar system.

The corona's lightning-like tentacles
grasp at space; their glow
dances in our eyes,
all of us aware of our own tininess,
all captivated and connected

. . . for those
tiny
precious
minutes.

In the crowd is one

           tiny

                precious . . .

                        you.

Arms spread wide
in the sweet, cool grass,
under a velvet panorama,
you come face-to-face with
the splendor of the universe

. . . for a few beautiful minutes.

But it cannot last.
All shows must end.

The moon glides on.
The sun reemerges,
reclaiming her daytime throne.

As light creeps back to Earth,
we look around at one another.
Once strangers, now we are friends—
people who, together, glimpsed the extraordinary.

Speechless, we smile,
we hug and high-five,
and we remember all that we saw . . .

. . . for a few beautiful minutes.

What Is a Solar Eclipse?

A *total solar eclipse* occurs when the sun, moon, and Earth line up perfectly, so that the moon appears to block all of the sun's light from certain places on Earth. Though the sun is about four hundred times wider than the moon, the moon is about four hundred times closer to Earth, allowing it to sometimes block out the sun. The places on Earth where people can see a total solar eclipse—called the *path of the totality*—can stretch for thousands of miles in a narrow band. The *totality*—or time of total darkness—will last about four minutes in most places.

While total solar eclipses are visible from someplace on Earth about once every eighteen months, they only happen about once every four hundred years in the same place—like where you live. A total solar eclipse will be visible in parts of North America on April 8, 2024. Another total solar eclipse will darken parts of Europe on August 12, 2026.

Annular eclipses, which occur when part of the sun remains visible around the edges of the moon, are more common than total eclipses.

Selected Resources

"Eclipse 101." NASA. https://eclipse2017.nasa.gov/faq.

Espenak, Fred. "Solar Eclipses 2021–2030." NASA. https://eclipse.gsfc.nasa.gov/SEdecade/SEdecade2021.html.

Mika, Anna. "Build a Sunspot Viewer." *National Geographic*. https://www.nationalgeographic.org/activity/build-a-sunspot-viewer/.

"What to See During an Eclipse." Exploratorium. https://www.exploratorium.edu/eclipse/what-to-see-during-eclipse.

Timeline of an Eclipse

The length of a total solar eclipse changes depending on the eclipse and your location within the path of the totality, but they all follow the same pattern. Here's what to expect!

Darkening skies (often an hour or more)
- The eclipse begins when the moon starts moving in front of the sun. The sky might not look very different yet.
- <u>Looking directly at the sun, even during an eclipse, can permanently damage your eyes!</u> Use a sun viewer or solar glasses to watch the sun's shape appear to change as the moon moves in front of it.
- Search for crescent shapes in the shadows of trees.
- As the moon moves farther in front of the sun, you may notice the sky growing darker.

A few minutes before total darkness
- Shortly before the sky goes totally dark, you may see a "sunset" that goes all the way around the horizon.
- Animals may begin nighttime activities. Listen for chirping crickets!
- In the last moment before the totality, you may see a "diamond ring" as the last rays of sunlight shine around the moon. It will look like a large empty circle (the "ring") with a small bright circle on one side (the "diamond").

Totality (often 2–5 minutes)
- <u>This is the only time you can safely view the eclipse without a sun viewer or solar glasses.</u>
- The sky will be dark except for the sun's corona—or outer atmosphere—which will appear to shine around the moon.
- Zip up your jacket! Temperatures can drop up to fifteen degrees Fahrenheit (about eight degrees Celsius) during the totality.

A few minutes after total darkness
- <u>Make sure you use your solar glasses or sun viewer to watch the rest of the eclipse.</u>
- As the moon moves past the sun, a second "diamond ring" effect may be visible.

Lightening skies (often an hour or more)
- The sun's seemingly changing shape may look like mirror images of the shapes you observed during the first half of the eclipse.
- The sky will gradually lighten until the moon has moved completely past the sun. At this point, the eclipse is over.
- Give your friends and family members a high five!

How to Build a Sun Viewer

Don't have solar glasses? With the help of an adult, you can build your own sun viewer to safely watch a solar eclipse.

Materials

Cereal box	Aluminum foil
White paper	Needle or pushpin
Pencil	Scissors
Tape	

Make the viewing screen

1. Place an empty cereal box upright on top of the white paper. Using a pencil, trace the shape of the bottom of the box onto the paper.

2. Cut out the rectangle along the traced outline.

3. Tape the paper rectangle to the inside of the bottom of the box. This will be your viewing screen.

Make the pinhole

1. Cut a small hole on the right side of the top of the box.

2. Tape a piece of aluminum foil over the hole. Make sure the foil is tight and no light can get in around the sides.

3. Use a needle or pushpin to make a small hole in the middle of the foil.

Make the eyehole

1. Cut another small hole on the left side of the top of the box. This is where you will look inside.

Enjoy!

1. Turn your back to the sun. Maneuver the pinhole so it is pointing at the sun as you look inside the box through the eyehole.

2. Keep moving the box until you see the shape of the sun on the viewing screen (the rectangular piece of paper). It should look like a small white circle.

3. Watch this shape change during the eclipse!

Don't forget! During the totality (time of total darkness)—and when an adult says it is safe— you can view the eclipse without solar glasses or a sun viewer. This will only last about 2–5 minutes. During the rest of the eclipse, use your sun viewer to protect your eyes.